THE USBORNE

FIRST THOUSAND WORDS

IN ARABIC

With easy pronunciation guide

D1338693

Heather Amery

Illustrated by Stephen Cartwright

Arabic language consultant: Adi Budeiri

Editor: Lisa Watts; Designer (revised edition): Andy Griffin

Translation and typesetting by y2ktranslations and Mouna Hammad

On every double page with pictures,
there is a little yellow duck to look for.
Can you find it?

About this book

This book provides a fun and engaging way for beginners to learn Arabic. On most of the pages, large, colourful panoramic scenes are surrounded with small pictures labelled with their names in Arabic.

Saying the words

Each Arabic word is also written in Roman letters, to show you how to pronounce it. Reading the words while looking at the pictures will help you remember them, and you can test yourself by looking for and naming the objects in the panoramic scenes. You can even practise forming simple sentences to talk about the pictures.

Arabic alphabet

At the back of the book there is a guide to the Arabic alphabet and a list of all the Arabic words with their pronunciation guides and meanings in English. Arabic is written from right to left and there are several sounds for which there are no equivalents in English. The pronunciation guides will help you, but the best way to learn how to say the words is to listen to a native Arabic speaker.

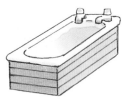

مغطس
maghtas

صابون
saboon

حنفيّة
hanafiyya

ورق حمّام
waraq hammam

فُرشة أسنان
furshat asnan

ماء
ma'

مرحاض
mirhad

سفَنجة
sfinja

مغَسلة
maghsaleh

دوش
doosh

منشَفة
manshafa

المنزل
el-manzil

سرير
sareer

 hammam **حمّام**

salon **صَالون**

معجون أسنان
ma''joun asnan

راديو
radio

مخدة
makhada

قُرص مُدمَج
qurs mudmaj

سجادة
sujjada

كنبة kanabay

4

كُرسي
kursi

لحاف
lihaf

مِشْط
musht

شرشف
sharshaf

بساطة
bisata

خزانة
khazana

غرفة نوم
ghurfat nawm

مخدة نوم
makhadat nawm

خزانة جوارير
khazanat jawareer

مِرآة
mir'a

فُرشة شعر
furshat sha"r

قِنديل
qandeel

مُلصقات
mulsaqat

مَدخَل
madkhal

علاقة
"allaqa

هاتف
hatef

رادييتير
radiatur

مُسجل فيديو
musajjel video

جَريدة
jareeda

طاولة
tawila

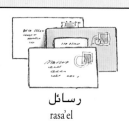
رسائل
rasa'el

درج
daraj

5

المطبخ
el matbakh

ثلاجة
thallaja

أكواب
akwab

ساعة حائط
sa''at ha'et

سكملة
skamla

معالق صغيرة
ma''aleq sagheera

مفتاح الكهرباء
miftah el kahraba

مسحوق غسيل
mas-houq ghaseel

مفتاح
miftah

باب
baab

مغسلة
maghsaleh

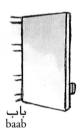

مكنسة كهربائية
mukunsa kahraba'eya

طناجر
tanaajer

شوك
shuwak

مريول
maryool

طاولة الكوي
tawilat el kawi

زبالة
zibala

إبريق غلي
ibreeq ghali

سكاكين
sakakeen

مكنسة خشنة
mukunsa khashina

خرقة
khirqa

بلاط صيني
balat sini

مكنسة
mukunsa

غسالة
ghassaleh

مجرود
majrood

جرار
jarrar

صحون صغيرة
suhoun sagheera

مقلاة
maqla

فرن
furun

ملاعق خشب
mala"eq khashab

صحون
suhoun

مكواة
mikwa

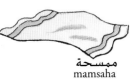
ممسحة
mamsaha

فناجين
fanajeen

علبة كبريت
"ulbat kibrit

فرشة
fursha

طاسات
tasat

خزانة حائط
khazanat ha'et

7

عربة يد
"arabet yad

خلية نحل
khaliyat nahel

حلزون
halazoon

طوب
toob

حمامة
hamama

مجرفة
majrafa

أم علي
um "ali

زبالة
zibala

بزر
bizr

كوخ
kukh

البستان
el bustan

مرش
mirrash

دودة أرض
dudet ard

أزهار
azhar

رشاش ماء
rashash ma'

مجرفة
majrafa

دبور
dabbour

8

نحلة
nahla

مسطرين
mastareen

عظمة
"athma

سياج
siyaj

شوكة
shawka

مقص الحشيش
miqass el hasheesh

ممر
mammar

أوراق شجر
awraq shajar

شجرة
shajara

دخان
dukhan

دودة
dudah

مشط
musht

عش
"ush

عصى
"usy

بيت بلاستيك
beit plastik

أعشاب
a"shab

عربة أطفال
"arabat atfal

سلم
sullam

نار
nar

أنبوب سقي
anboob saqi

9

الورشـة
el warsha

براغي صغيرة
baraghi sagheera

ملزمة
malzama

ورق زجاج
waraq zujaj

مقدَح
miqdah

سـلم
sullam

منشار
munshar

نشارة
nishara

تقويم
taqweem

صندوق عدة
sundouq "idda

مفك
mafak

لوح خشب
lawh khashab

نجارة
nijara

موس
moose

قوس
qaws

مظلة هبوط
mithalat huboot

مركب شراعي
markab shira"i

أصابع ألوان
asabe" alwan

مدحلة
midhala

أقنعة
aqni"a

سيارة سباق
sayyarat sibaq

حصان هزاز
hisan hazzaz

حصالة
hassala

غلل
ghulal

عرائس
"ara'es

بيانو
piano

رواد فضاء
ruwwad fada'

رافعة
rafi"a

ملتينة
malteenah

بندقية
bunduqiyya

جنود معدنية
junood ma"daniya

صندوق ألوان
sandooq alwan

صاروخ
sarookh

15

مراجيح
marajeeh

حوض رمل
hawd raml

نزهة
nuzha

طيارة ورق
tayyarat waraq

بوظة
bootha

كلب
kalb

حاجز
hajez

طريق
tareeq

ضفدع
dufda"

مزلقة
mizlaqa

الحديقة العامة

el hadeeqa el "amma

مقعد
maq"ad

فرخ الضفضع
farkh ed-dufda"

بحيرة
buhaira

أحذية تزلج
ahthiyat tazzaluj

عشبة
"ushba

رضيع
radee"

لوحة تزلج
lawhat tazzluj

تراب
turab

عربة أطفال
"arabat atfal

زحلوقة
zahlouka

أطفال
atfal

دراجة ثلاثية
darraja thulathiya

عصافير
"asafeer

سياج
siyaj

كرة
kura

قارب
qareb

خيطان
khitan

بريكة
burreika

فرخ البط
farkh el batt

حبل القفز
habl elqafz

شجر
shajar

حوض زريعة
hawd zira"a

وز
waz

رسن
rasan

بط
batt

حديقة الحيوانات

hadiqat el-hayawanat

جناح
janah

صقر
saqr

جاموس البحر
jamoos el-bahr

بندا
panda

غوريلا
ghorilla

كفوف
kufuf

قنغر
kanghur

خفاش
khaffash

قرد
qird

ذنب
thanab

ذئب
th'ib

صخرة جليد
sakhrat jaleed

بطريق
batreeq

دُب
dub

تمساح
timsah

ريش
reesh

بجع
baja"

نعامة
na"ama

دلفين
dolfin

أسـد
asad

أشبال
ashbal

زرافة
zarafa

18

خيام
khiyam

قناة
qana

جذوع الشجر
juthoo" esh-shajar

قَرية
qarya

فَراشة ليل
farashat layl

جِسر
jisr

مركب بضائع
markab bada'e"

شلّال
shallal

بومة
booma

نفق
nafaq

جرو الثعلب
jarou eth-tha"lab

خُلند
khlund

صيّاد سمَك
sayyad samak

صخور
sukhoor

ضفضعتين
dufda"teen

قطار
qitar

بيت منقول
bayt manqool

تلّة
talla

23

متبنة
matbaneh

المزرعة
el mazra"a

ديك
deek

كَلب الراعي
kalb er-ra"i

بَط
batt

حُملان
humlan

بِركة
birka

صيصان
seesan

مخزن القمح
makhzan el qamh

حظيرة الخنازير
hatherat el khanazeer

ثور
thawr

فرخ البط
farkh el batt

قن دجاج
qunn dajaj

جرارة
jarrara

أوزات
awzat

شاحنة صهريج
shahinat sahreej

حظيرة
hatheera

وحل
wahl

عربة
"araba

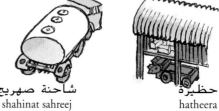

24

مزارع
muzare"

حقل
haql

دجاج
dajaj

عجل
"ijl

سياج
siyaj

سرج
sarj

حظيرة بقر
hatherat baqar

بقرة
baqara

محراث
mihrath

بستان فاكهة
bustan fakiha

إسطبل
istabel

خنانيص
khananees

راعية
ra"iya

ديوك حبش
duyuk habash

فزاعة
fazza"a

مزرعة
mazra"a

حشيش
hasheesh

خرفان
khirfan

حزم التبن
huzam et-tibn

حصان
hissan

خنازير
khanazeer

25

مركب شراعي
markab shira"i

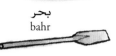

بحر
bahr

مجداف
mijdaf

منار
manar

مجرفة
mijrafa

سطل
sattel

نجمة البحر
najmat el bahr

قلعة رملية
qal"a ramliya

شمسية
shamsiya

علم
"alam

بحار
bahhar

شاطىء البحر

shate' el-bahr

صدفة
sadafa

سرطان
saratan

نورس
nawras

جزيرة
jazeera

قارب سريع
qareb saree"

تزلّج مائي
tazalluj ma'ee

الطَبيب
el tabeeb

شبشب
shibsheb

حاسوب
hasoob

ضماد لاصق
dimad laseq

موز
mawz

عِنَب
"inab

سلّة
salla

ألعاب
al"ab

أجاص
ajas

بطاقات
bitaqat

حفاض
hifad

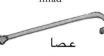
عصا
"asa

تلفزيون
levizyon

قَميص نوم
qamees nawm

لباس نوم
libas nawm

برتقالة
burtqala

مناديل ورق
manadeel waraq

رواية مُصوّرة
riwaya mussawara

قاعة الإنتظار
qa"at el intithar

31

الحَفلة
el hafla

هدايا
hadaya

بالون
balloon

شوكولاتة
shokolata

ملبس
mlabass

نافذة
nafitha

ألعاب نارية
al"ab nariyya

وِشاح
wishah

كَعكَة
ka"ka

مصاصة
massasa

شَمعَة
sham"a

ورق زينة
waraq zena

ألعَاب
al"ab

32

ماندالينة
mandalina

سُجُق
sujuq

شَريط مُسَجّل
shareet mussajel

نَقانَق
naqaneq

شرائح البَطاطا
shara'eh el batata

أزياء تَنَكُرية
azya' tannakuriyya

كرز
karaz

عَصير فَواكِه
"aseer fawakih

توت
toot

فَراوُلة
farawla

لمبة
lamba

شَطيرَة
shateera

زُبدة
zubda

بِسكوت
baskoot

جبنة
jubna

خبز
khubz

غطاء الطاولة
ghita' et-tawila

33

البقالة
el baqqala

غرابفروت
grapefroot

جَزَر
jazar

قَرنبيط
qarnabeet

كُراث
kurath

فِطر
fitr

خِيار
khiyar

ليمون
laimoon

كَرَفْس
karafs

مشمش
mishmish

بَطيخ
batteekh

حقيبة
haqeeba

جبنة

خضر وفواكه

بَصَل
basal

ملفوف
malfoof

خوخ
khookh

خس
khass

بزيلا
bazilla

بندورة
bandoura

34

بيض
bayd

برقوق
barqooq

طحين
taheen

ميزان
mizan

مرطبانات
martabanat

لحمة
lahma

أناناس
ananas

لبن رائب
laban ra'eb

سلّة
salla

زُجاجات
zujajat

حقيبة يد
haqibat yad

كيس نقود
kees nqood

نُقود
nuqood

مُعلَّبات
mu"allabat

بَطاطا
batata

سبانخ
sabanekh

فاصولية
fasoolya

صندوق الدفع
sundooq ed-daf"

قرع
qar"

عربة
"araba

35

الأكل

el akl

غذاء
ghatha'

فطور
futoor

بيض مسلوق
bayd maslooq

قهوة
qahwa

بيض مقلى
bayd maqli

خُبز مُحمّص
khubz muhamas

مُربى
murabba

قِشدَة
qishda

حَليب
haleeb

حُبوب
huboob

شوكولاته ساخنة
shokolata sakhina

سُكَّر
sukkar

شاي
shay

عَسَل
'asal

ملح
malh

فلفل
filfil

إبريق شاي
ibreeq shay

فطائر
fata'er

أقراص خبز
aqras khubz

36

عَشاء
"asha'

لَحمة
lahma

شوربة
shoraba

عُجّة
"ujja

سَلَطة
salata

عصي
"usi

برغر
burger

دجاجة
dajaja

صلصة بندورة
salsat bandoura

أرُز
arruz

معكرونة
ma"karona

بطاطا مهروسة
batata mahroosa

بتزة
pitza

بطاطا مقلية
batata maqliyya

تحليَات
tahliyat

37

أنا
ana

شَعَر
sha"r

رأس
ra's

وَجه
wajh

ذِراع
thira"

كوع
koo"

بَطن
batn

أصابع الرِجل
asabe" ar-rijil

رِجل
rijel

سَاق
saq

رُكبة
rukba

حاجب
hajib

عَين
"ayn

أُنف
anf

خَدّ
khadd

فَم
famm

شَفاه
shiffah

أسنان
asnan

لِسان
lisan

ذَقن
thaqn

أذن
uthn

رَقبة
raqaba

كَتَف
katef

صَدر
sadr

ظَهر
thaher

خَلف
khalf

يَدّ
yad

إبهام
ibham

أصابع
asabe"

38

مَلبس
malbas

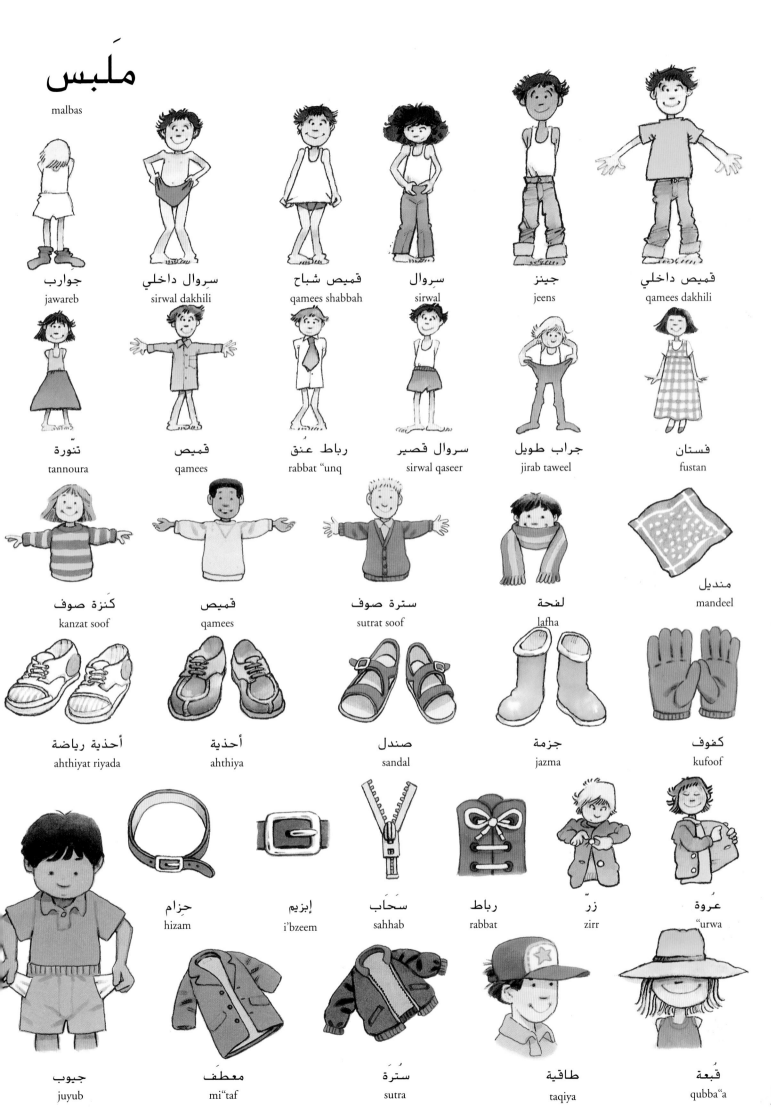

جوارب
jawareb

سروال داخلي
sirwal dakhili

قميص شباح
qamees shabbah

سروال
sirwal

جينز
jeens

قميص داخلي
qamees dakhili

تنّورة
tannoura

قميص
qamees

رباط عُنق
rabbat "unq

سروال قصير
sirwal qaseer

جراب طويل
jirab taweel

فستان
fustan

كَنزة صوف
kanzat soof

قميص
qamees

سترة صوف
sutrat soof

لفحة
lafha

منديل
mandeel

أحذية رياضة
ahthiyat riyada

أحذية
ahthiya

صندل
sandal

جزمة
jazma

كفوف
kufoof

حِزام
hizam

إبزيم
i'bzeem

سَحَاب
sahhab

رباط
rabbat

زِرّ
zirr

عُروة
"urwa

جيوب
juyub

معطَف
mi"taf

سَترة
sutra

طافية
taqiya

قُبعة
qubba"a

39

الناس
en-nas

طبّاخ
tabbakh

راقصة
raqisa

راقص
raqes

مُمثِّل
mumathel

مُمثِّلة
mumathela

مُغنّي
mughani

مغنية
mughaniya

رائد فضاء
ra'ed fada'

لحام
lahham

رجال الشرطة/ نساء الشرطة
rijal esh-shurta / nisa' esh-shurta

نَجّار
najjar

رجُل إطفاء
rajul itfa'

فنانة
fannana

قاضي
qadi

ميكانيكي
mikaniki

ميكانيكية
mikanikiya

40

حلاق
hallaq

سائِقة شاحنة
sa'eqat shahina

قائد حافلة
qa'ed hafila

نادِل
nadel

نادلة
nadila

ساعي البَريد
sa"i el bareed

طبيبة أسنان
tabeebat asnan

غواص
ghawwas

دهان
dahhan

خبّازة
khabbaza

العائلة
al "a'ila

إبن
ibn

أخ
akh

إبنة
ibna

أُخت
ukht

أُم
umm

زوجة
zawja

أب
abb

زوج
zawj

عمّة
"amma
خالة
khala

عمّ
"amm
خال
khal

إبن عمّ
ibn "amm

إبن خال
ibn khal

جدّ
jadd

جدّة
jadda

41

الأعمال اليومية

el a"mal el yawmiyah

إبتسام
ibtisam

بكاء
buka'

تفكير
tafkeer

سمع
sama"

ضَحك
dahk

قبض
qabd

رمي
ramy

كسر
kasr

رسم
rasm

كتابة
kitaba

قطع
qat"

قص
qass

أكل
akl

تكلم
takkalum

حفر
hafr

حمل
haml

شرب
shurb

صنع
sun"

قفز
qafz

رقص
raqs

غسل
ghasl

حباكة
hiyaka

زحف
zahf

42

الأعياد
el-a"yad

عيد ميلاد
"eed milad

هدية
hadiyya

بطاقات عيد ميلاد
bitaqat "eed milad

شمعة
sham"a

كعكة عيد ميلاد
ka"kat "eed milad

عطلة
"utla

يوم الزفاف
yawm ez-zafaf

آلة تصوير
alat tasweer

وصيفة
waseefa

عروس
"aroos

عريس
"arees

مصور
musawwir

عيد الميلاد
"eed el milad

أيل
ayl

بابا نويل
baba nowel

زلاجة
zallaja

شجرة عيد الميلاد
shajarat "eed el milad

47

أحوال الطقس

ahwal et-taqs

شمس
shams

غيوم
ghuyum

سماء
sama'

مظلة
mithala

مطر
matar

برق
barq

سديم
sediim

ثلج
thalj

ندى
nada

ريح
reeh

ضباب
dabaab

جليد
jaleed

قوس قزح
qaws quzah

الفصول

el fusool

ربيع
rabee"

صيف
sayf

خريف
khareef

شتاء
shita'

48

حيوانات أليفة

hayawanat aleefa

بيطرية
baytariyya

مرنب
marnab

بيت الكلب
bayt el kalb

بودغريغر
budgerigar

خنزير هندي
khanzeer hindi

جرو
jaru

كلب
kalb

أكل
akl

ببغاء
babbagha'

منقار
munqar

كنار
kinar

قفص
qafas

أرنب
arnab

هرة
hirra

سلّة
salla

هريرة
huraira

حليب
haleeb

سمك ذهبي
samak thahabee

فار
fa'r

49

الرياضة
er-riyadha

كُرة السلة
kurat es-sallah

تجديف
tajdeef

لوحة تزلج
lawhat tazalluj

إبحار شراعي
ibhar shira"i

لوحة شراعية
lawha shira"iyya

مضرب
madrab

كريكت
kriket

كَراتي
karate

تنيس أرضي
tennis ardi

كرة قدم أمريكية
kurat qadam amerikiya

جُمباز
jumbaz

كرة
kura

مضرب
madrab

سنارة
sunnara

صيد سمك
sayd samak

طعم
tu"m

رقص
raqs

كرة القاعدة
kurat el qa"ida

رُغبي
rugby

غوص
ghaws

مسبح
masbah

سباحة
sibaha

سباق الركض
sibaq er-rakd

رمي بالقوس
ramy bil qaws

مرمى
marma

طيران شراعي
tayaran shira"i

خوذة
khootha

عدو
"ado

دراجات هوائية
darrajat haw'iyya

تسلق
tassalluq

جودو
judo

حصان
hissan

فرس
faras

خزانة حائط
khazanat ha'et

كرة القدم
kurat el-qadam

فروسية
furusiyya

غرفة غيار
ghurfat ghayar

كرة الريشة
kurat er-reesha

تنيس الطاولة
tennis et-tawila

مزالج جليد
mazalej jaleed

تزلج جليدي
tazalluj jaleedi

عصا تزلج
"asa tazalluj

مقعد هوائي
miq"ad hawa'ee

مَزالج
mazalej

تزلج على الثلج
tazalluj "ala eth-thalj

مصارعة سومو
musar"at sumo

51

الألوان
el alwan

برتقالى
burtuqali

أخضر
akhdar

أسود
aswad

رمادي
ramadi

أحمر
ahmar

بنى
bunnee

أبيض
abyad

أزرق
azraq

وردي
wardi

بنفسجي
banafsaji

أصفر
asfar

الأشكال
el ashkal

مستطيل
mustateel

دائرة
da'era

معين
ma''een

مخروط
makhroot

نجمة
najma

مكعب
muka''ab

بيضي
baydi

مثلث
muthalath

مربع
murraba''

هلال
hilal

الأعداد

١	واحد wahid	
٢	إثنان ithnan	
٣	ثلاثة thalatha	
٤	أربعة arba"a	
٥	خمسة khamsa	
٦	ستة sitta	
٧	سبعة sab"a	
٨	ثمانية thamaniya	
٩	تسعة tis"a	
١٠	عشرة "ashara	
١١	أحد عشر ihada "ashar	
١٢	إثنا عشر ithna "ashar	
١٣	ثلاثة عشر thalathata "ashar	
١٤	أربعة عشر arba"ata "ashar	
١٥	خمسة عشر khamsata "ashar	
١٦	ستة عشر sittata "ashar	
١٧	سبعة عشر sab"ata "ashar	
١٨	ثمانية عشر thamaniyata "ashar	
١٩	تسعة عشر tis"ata "ashar	
٢٠	عشرون "ishroon	

53

مدينة الملاهي
madinat el malahi

دوارة
dawara

ممسحة أقدام
mamsahat aqdam

مزلقة عملاقة
mizlaqa "imlaqa

دولاب الكبير
doolab el kabeer

قطارالرعب
qitar er-ru"b

فشار
fushar

حلقات
halaqaat

جبال روسية
jibal roosiyya

رمي البندقية
ramy el bunduqiya

سيارات متصادمة
sayyarat mutasadima

غزَل البنات
ghazl el banat

54

First published in 2003 by Usborne Publishing Ltd, Usborne House, 83-85 Saffron Hill, London EC1N 8RT, England. www.usborne.com. Based on a previous title first published in 1979 and revised in 1995. Copyright © 2003, 1995, 1979 Usborne Publishing Ltd.

Fasting

Every year Muslim people all over the world celebrate Ramadan. We observe our most important holiday with fasting, prayer, and charity.

Prayer

< These are pages of the Cairo Qur'an, which was made for the Sultan of Morocco in the 18th century.

Charity

Ramadan is a holy time

because many years ago, during
the month of Ramadan, our
prophet Muhammad received
the words of Allah (God).
These teachings became the
Qur'an, our holy book.

Ramadan is the ninth month
of our year. Because of the
lunar calendar we use, it can
take place in spring, summer,
fall, or winter.

When we see the crescent moon
of the month of Ramadan, we
know it is time to begin.

It is time
to begin.

During Ramadan, adults and teenagers fast. For a whole month we do not eat or drink anything from sunrise until sunset. Not even a sip of water or a piece of gum. Children don't have to fast, but many of us try to fast part of the time. We practice for when we are older.

Muslims fast during Ramadan to purify ourselves. We also fast so we know what it feels like to be poor and hungry all the time.

Muslims fast during Ramadan.

< *Abu Mofid Kosum reads the Qur'an to a young friend outside a cabin he uses for meditation in the Galilee region of Israel.*

We eat sahur.

During Ramadan, we get up very early in the morning, while it is still dark. Normally we would think of it as the middle of the night! We eat *sahur* to have energy for the day. Muslims all over the world eat different kinds of food at sahur. But we mostly eat cereal, bread, honey, jam, pancakes, eggs, cheese, tea, and juice.

> *An extended family in Basra, Iraq, enjoys sahur together.*

∨ Elementary-school children in Jakarta, Indonesia, paint symbolic landscape pictures of Islam during Ramadan.

It is hard to fast.

After sahur we wash

and say our morning prayers.
It is still dark. Sometimes we
go back to bed for a little to
rest. Then we go to school or
to work. It is hard to fast while
we go to school and play sports.
It is difficult for grown-ups to
work while they are fasting.
But we try to live life as usual
during Ramadan.

∧ *These girls in a suburb of Sydney, Australia, practice their karate twice a week, even during Ramadan.*

At the end of every day,

after sunset, we eat another meal.
It is called *iftar*. We love to eat with
our grandparents, aunts, uncles,
and cousins, if they live close by. If
not, we eat with friends. We break
our fast by drinking water and eating
some dates. That is how Muhammad
broke his fast. Then we eat delicious
and healthful foods. We try not to
eat too much!

∧ *A cannon goes off at sunset
on Mount Noqum in Sanaa,
Yemen, to signal the end of
the fast for the day.*

> *Friends eat iftar
together at a party in
Potomac, Maryland.*

12

We break our fast.

During Ramadan we read the Qur'an. Some people read it from the beginning to the end. That takes the whole month. We think about God. And we think about what Muhammad, our prophet, taught us. He taught us to believe in God, to pray, and to think of others.

We think about God.

< In Sharjah, United Arab Emirates, a boy carries food for iftar provided by the Red Crescent, which feeds the needy during Ramadan.

> A boy prepares food to share for iftar at a mosque in Karachi, Pakistan.

We think of those who are hungry.

We give to the needy.

We give money to people who are poor or have suffered a tragedy. We think of those who are hungry every day, and we invite others to join us for iftar. Sometimes we invite our non-Muslim friends to join us.

^ Men kneel in prayer on a rooftop in New Delhi, India, on a Friday evening during Ramadan.

We ask for forgiveness.

Toward the end of Ramadan is the Night of Power. We spend extra hours in prayer. Sometimes we stay all night at the mosque.

At this time we forgive all who have hurt us. We ask for forgiveness from those we have hurt. We promise to serve God and to do good deeds. We promise to be better people.

< In Philadelphia, Pennsylvania, a man prays at a mosque on the last day of Ramadan. He is joined at the mosque by Muslims from West Africa, the Middle East, Europe, and other parts of the U.S.

It is Eid al-Fitr!

U.S. postage stamp ∧

< Women dance to celebrate the end of Ramadan and the beginning of Eid al-Fitr in Beijing, China.

> This man in Srinagar, India, hopes people will buy his beautiful cakes to celebrate Eid. The writing on the cake means Happy Eid.

We know it is the end of

Ramadan when we see a new crescent moon. That means it is a new month called *Shawwal*. And it is time to celebrate. It is Eid al-Fitr!

21

A boy waits his turn on a carousel at an Eid festival in Balkh, Afghanistan.

22

We visit family and friends.

> In Nepal, girls decorate their hands with henna in celebration of Eid al-Fitr.

∨ Women in Lahore, Pakistan, buy colorful bangle bracelets to wear on Eid.

We put on new clothes.

We visit with family and friends. We especially pay our respects to our oldest relatives. We give and receive little gifts and money. We share meals of delicious food. We even have carnivals and fairs.

After prayers, two boys hug each other outside the Jama Masjid, or Friday Mosque, in New Dehli, India.